AF687957

CONTENTS

CONTENTS

INTRODUCTION

Welcome to The Fortune Formula Guide! Whether you're just beginning your financial journey or looking to optimize your wealth-building strategies, this guide provides actionable steps that anyone can take to secure a better economic future. With a focus on mindset, saving, investing, and side hustles, you'll learn how to create a plan that leads to lasting wealth.

This book is packed with insights backed by research and real-world success stories, so you can feel confident in the steps you take toward your financial independence. Remember: building wealth isn't about luck–it's about taking deliberate actions over time.

CHAPTER 1: 5 PROVEN STEPS TO BUILD WEALTH RIGHT NOW

MINDSET & HABITS OF WEALTHY PEOPLE

To build wealth, the first step is shifting your mindset. Research shows that mindset plays a critical role in financial success. According to a study from the Journal of Personality and Social Psychology, individuals with a "growth mindset" are more likely to succeed in wealth-building endeavors. They see challenges as opportunities to learn and grow, rather than obstacles that cannot be overcome (Dweck, 2006).

Key Principles:

- Delayed Gratification: Wealthy people understand the power of delayed gratification. The marshmallow experiment, conducted by Walter Mischel at Stanford University, found that children who were able to wait for a larger reward were more likely to succeed later in life (Mischel, 2014).
- Continuous Learning: Self-made millionaires are avid readers. In fact, The Millionaire Next Door, a well-known book based on research by Thomas Stanley and William Danko, found that the average millionaire reads 5+ books per month (Stanley & Danko, 1996).
- Networking & Relationships: According to Think and Grow Rich by Napoleon Hill, 85% of success comes from your ability to work with others. Building strong relationships can provide opportunities that propel you forward in your wealth journey.

Action Step:

Start by changing your mindset. For the next 30 days, track your thoughts and decisions related to money. When you're about to make a purchase, ask yourself, “Is this a long-term investment in my wealth or a short-term satisfaction?”

CREATING MULTIPLE STREAMS OF INCOME

A critical aspect of wealth-building is having multiple sources of income. According to a report by the Bureau of Labor Statistics, the average millionaire has at least 7 sources of income. Diversifying your income streams helps protect against job loss and allows you to leverage different opportunities. Research shows that millionaires are less likely to rely on just one income source. A study by Deloitte found that 60% of high-net-worth individuals have more than one income stream, with many investing in stocks, real estate, or starting side businesses.

Action Step:

Identify one new stream of income you can start today. It could be as simple as freelancing your skills, starting an online store, or investing a small amount in stocks. The key is to get started now.

DEBT MANAGEMENT

High-interest debt is a barrier to building wealth. A study by NerdWallet found that the average American household with credit card debt pays over $1,000 annually in interest. High-interest debt, like credit cards, can significantly stunt your financial growth.

Key Principles:

- The Snowball Method: Paying off smaller debts first creates momentum. My brother, Luis, managed to pay off $37,512 and become debt-free in 18 months.
- The Avalanche Method: Paying off high-interest debt first saves money in the long term, and it's backed by research from NerdWallet, which recommends the avalanche method to minimize interest payments.

Action Step:

Review all your debt. Identify the most urgent debts (i.e., high-interest credit cards) and decide on which strategy (snowball or avalanche) you'll use to pay them off. Start by focusing all extra funds on one debt.

BUDGETING & TRACKING EXPENSES

Without a budget, your financial goals can feel like a distant dream. A study published by The Journal of Financial Counseling and Planning found that individuals with a written budget are more likely to succeed financially than those who don't (Xiao & O'Neill, 2016). Budgeting helps you track where your money goes and allows you to allocate funds toward savings and investments.

Practical Tips for Budgeting:

- The 50/30/20 Rule: A well-known rule that's recommended by financial experts. By allocating 50% to essentials, 30% to wants, and 20% to savings and debt repayment, you can maintain balance while building wealth.
- Use Apps to Track: Apps like Mint, YNAB (You Need a Budget), and Personal Capital have been shown to help people save more effectively by providing clear visual representations of their finances.

Action Step:

Create your budget using a simple spreadsheet or a budgeting app. Track your expenses for the next 30 days to understand where your money is going and identify areas to cut back.

SETTING SHORT-TERM AND LONG-TERM GOALS

Setting clear financial goals is crucial. According to a study from Harvard Business School, people who set specific goals are 50% more likely to achieve them than those who don't. Wealthy individuals set both short-term (1-2 years) and long-term (5+ years) goals, which allows them to take deliberate steps toward achieving their financial dreams.

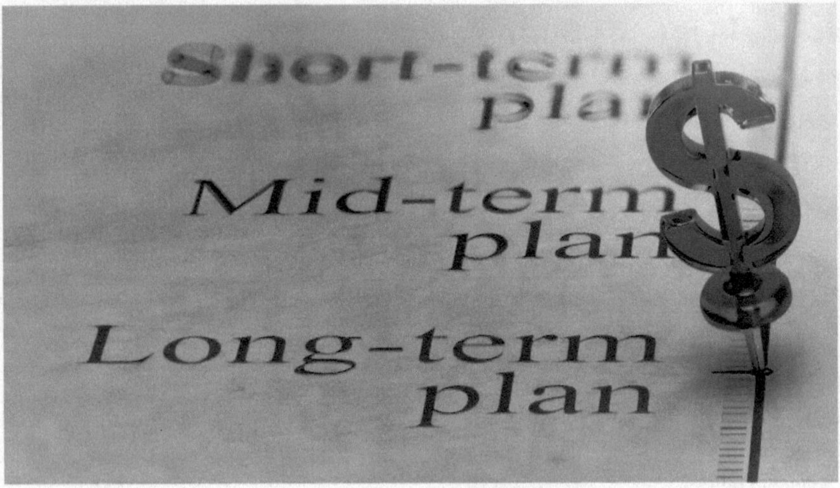

Action Step:

Write down at least one short-term and one long-term financial goal. Be specific: "I will save $5,000 for an emergency fund by the end of the year."

CHAPTER 2: HOW TO SAVE & INVEST YOUR FIRST $10K

BUILDING YOUR FIRST EMERGENCY FUND

The first step in securing your financial future is building an emergency fund. A study by Bankrate found that 25% of Americans have no emergency savings, and 40% of people would struggle to cover a $400 unexpected expense. Building a solid emergency fund (3-6 months of living expenses) ensures you're prepared for life's surprises.

Why You Need an Emergency Fund:

- Peace of Mind: Knowing you have money set aside can reduce financial stress and anxiety. A study published by Psychological Science found that financial stress can impact overall well-being, making it harder to focus on other aspects of life (Gathergood, 2012).
- Avoid Debt: When you have an emergency fund, you're less likely to rely on high-interest credit cards to cover unexpected costs, which means fewer long-term financial burdens.

Action Step:

Start by saving $1,000 as quickly as you can. Once that's in place, continue saving until you have 3-6 months of expenses.

HOW TO SAVE EFFECTIVELY

Saving effectively doesn't require depriving yourself–it's about making conscious decisions. According to The National Bureau of Economic Research, individuals who automate their savings are more likely to save effectively because the process becomes effortless. You simply "pay yourself first" before anything else.

Tips for Effective Saving:

- Automate Your Savings: Studies show that individuals who automate their savings save more consistently (Shlomo Benartzi, 2012). Set up automatic transfers to your savings account every payday to build your fund with minimal effort.
- Cut Back on Luxuries: Reevaluate spending habits like expensive coffee runs or dining out. Redirect this money toward investments. The Bureau of Labor Statistics notes that an average family of four spends $3,000 per year on dining out. Consider cooking at home to redirect that money into savings.

Action Step:

Set up an automatic savings plan. For example, if you earn $3,000 per month, automate a $300 transfer to your savings account on payday.

How to Invest Your First $1,000 (Starting Small)

Once you've successfully saved your first $1,000, it's time to put that money to work! Investing is essential for growing wealth over time, as savings alone won't keep up with inflation or generate significant returns. Once you've successfully saved your first $1,000, it's time to put that money to work! Investing is essential for growing wealth over time, as savings alone won't keep up with inflation or generate significant returns.

Where to invest your first $1000:

- Low-Cost Index Funds & ETFs: Index funds and exchange-traded funds (ETFs) are designed to track the performance of major stock market indices (like the S&P 500). They have low fees and have historically provided solid long-term returns (around 7-10% annually on average). You can start by investing in ETFs through brokerage accounts like Vanguard, Fidelity, or Schwab.
- High-Yield Savings Accounts or Money Market Accounts: If you're risk-averse or want a safer place for your money as you get started, a high-yield savings account or money market account offers better interest rates than a traditional savings account. To get started, look for online banks offering rates of 2-3% APY or higher. Examples include Ally Bank, Marcus by Goldman Sachs, and Discover Bank.

Diversification - Spreading Risk:

As a beginner, don't put all your money into one investment. Diversifying – or spreading your investments across different asset classes – reduces risk and can help protect your portfolio from market volatility.

THE POWER OF COMPOUND INTEREST & SETTING INVESTMENT GOALS

One of the most powerful tools for building wealth over time is compound interest. This is when the money you earn from interest or investment gains starts to earn interest itself. The earlier you start investing, the more time your money has to compound and grow. The key takeaway: the longer your money is invested, the more it will grow. Starting early allows compound interest to work in your favor, which is why it's crucial to invest as soon as possible, even with smaller amounts.

Setting Investment Goals:

- Short-Term Goals (1-3 years): Example: "I want to save and invest $5,000 for a down payment on a car or home." Focus on safer investments like high-yield savings accounts, money market accounts, or short-term bonds to preserve your capital.
- Medium-Term Goals (3-5 years: Example: "I want to build a $10,000 emergency fund and grow my investments for retirement." At this stage, consider adding more stock-based investments or diversified ETFs. Balance risk and reward based on your comfort level.
- Long-Term Goals (5+ years): Example: "I want to save $100,000 for retirement by age 40." Focus on more aggressive investments like stocks, index funds, or even individual growth stocks. As your time horizon increases, you can afford to take on more risk.

The Smart Investment Habit

Instead of trying to time the market (which can be risky and unpredictable), dollar-cost averaging involves investing a fixed amount regularly, regardless of market conditions.

CHAPTER 3: SIDE HUSTLES THAT CAN MAKE YOU $100+ A DAY FREELANCING: SKILLS THAT PAY WELL

Freelancing is one of the easiest ways to start making money on the side. In fact, a study by Upwork shows that 59 million Americans participated in the gig economy in 2020. Freelancers earn an average of $28 per hour, and that can quickly add up to $100+ per day depending on the amount of work you take on.

High-Demand Freelance Skills:

- Writing and Copywriting: Companies are constantly in need of writers for blog posts, product descriptions, and marketing materials. The average freelance writer earns between $50–$100 per hour, depending on experience.
- Web Development: Coding is one of the highest-paying freelance skills. Full-stack developers can earn $60–$100 per hour.
- Graphic Design: If you're skilled in design tools like Adobe Illustrator or Canva, you can offer services for creating logos, websites, and marketing materials. Graphic designers can earn $30–$60 per hour.

Action Step:

Start by signing up on platforms like Upwork, Fiverr, or Freelancer. Offer a service that aligns with your skills, and set a goal to make at least $100 per day within the next month.

ONLINE COACHING OR CONSULTING

If you have expertise in a specific area, whether it's business, fitness, or personal finance, online coaching or consulting can be an excellent side hustle. According to a study by *Grand View Research*, the online coaching market is expected to grow to $20 billion by 2027, driven by increased demand for personal development.

How to Get Started:

- Identify Your Niche: Think about areas where you can add value. Whether it's helping people lose weight, improve their personal finances, or start a business, find a niche where people are willing to pay for your expertise.
- Build an Online Presence: Use social media platforms like Instagram, LinkedIn, or YouTube to build credibility and attract clients.
- Offer Packages: Create coaching packages that offer value, such as 1-on-1 sessions, group coaching, or digital products like ebooks or courses.

Action Step:

Create a simple website or social media profile showcasing your expertise. Offer free content initially (blog posts, videos, tips) to build your audience, then introduce paid services as you grow your reputation.

DROPSHIPPING & E-COMMERCE

Dropshipping allows you to sell products online without handling inventory. According to Statista, the global dropshipping market is projected to reach $557.9 billion by 2025. It's an easy way to get started with e-commerce, as the supplier ships products directly to customers, and you only pay for the items once you make a sale.

How to Get Started:

- Identify Your Niche**:** Think about areas where you can add value. Whether it's helping people lose weight, improve their personal finances, or start a business, find a niche where people are willing to pay for your expertise.
- Set Up an Online Store: Use platforms like Shopify or WooCommerce to build an e-commerce store with minimal upfront cost.
- Market Your Store: Use social media ads, influencer partnerships, and organic SEO to drive traffic to your store.

Action Step:

Choose a product or niche, create your online store, and set up a simple social media campaign to start attracting customers. Aim to generate at least $100 in sales daily by optimizing your ad targeting and product offerings.

AFFILIATE MARKETING

Affiliate marketing involves promoting other companies' products and earning a commission for each sale made through your referral. According to Forbes, the affiliate marketing industry is expected to surpass $12 billion in the next few years.

How It Works:

- Find Affiliate Programs: Join affiliate networks like Amazon Associates, ShareASale, or ClickBank, which offer thousands of products to promote.
- Build a Platform: Create a blog, YouTube channel, or social media account to review products and recommend services. As your audience grows, you can start earning a steady stream of passive income.
- Earn Passive Income: As people purchase products through your affiliate links, you'll earn commissions without having to do any additional work after setting up your content.

Action Step:

Start a blog or YouTube channel related to a niche you're passionate about, and sign up for affiliate programs. Post content that includes your affiliate links, and track your earnings.

VIRTUAL ASSISTANCE

Virtual assistants (VAs) provide administrative support to businesses remotely. According to Business News Daily, the demand for virtual assistants is growing, and many VAs earn $20–$50 per hour depending on their expertise.

What VAs Do:

- General Administration: Tasks like scheduling appointments, managing emails, and answering customer inquiries.
- Social Media Management: Creating posts, responding to comments, and managing social media accounts.
- Research: Conducting market research or gathering data for business decisions.

Action Step:

Offer your virtual assistance services on platforms like Belay, Time Etc., or Upwork. Specialize in one area, like social media management or email organization, to stand out from the competition.

CHAPTER 4: INVESTING YOUR WAY TO WEALTH

THE BASICS OF STOCK MARKET INVESTING

Investing in the stock market is one of the most powerful ways to grow wealth over time. According to a study by Dalbar, the average investor's returns are significantly lower than the overall market due to poor timing decisions and emotional investing. The S&P 500, a key benchmark of U.S. stocks, has returned an average of 10% per year over the past 90 years.

Types of Investments:

- Individual Stocks: Buying shares in individual companies can lead to significant returns, but it also carries higher risk. Research shows that diversified portfolios tend to outperform individual stock investments over time.
- Exchange-Traded Funds (ETFs): ETFs are a great option for beginner investors. They allow you to invest in a broad array of stocks without having to pick individual winners.
- Mutual Funds: Like ETFs, mutual funds pool money from multiple investors to buy a diversified set of stocks or bonds.

Action Step:

Start with ETFs or index funds to build a low-risk, diversified portfolio. Platforms like Vanguard, Fidelity, and Charles Schwab offer easy-to-use tools for beginner investors.

REAL ESTATE INVESTING

Real estate has long been considered a reliable way to build wealth. According to The National Association of Realtors, 90% of millionaires have some form of real estate in their portfolio.

Ways to Invest in Real Estate:

- Rental Properties: Buying rental properties can generate passive income through rent payments. This strategy requires capital upfront but can provide long-term cash flow.
- Real Estate Investment Trusts (REITs): REITs allow you to invest in real estate without owning property directly. They are traded like stocks and can provide consistent dividends.

Action Step:

If you're new to real estate, start by investing in a REIT or look into real estate crowdfunding platforms like Fundrise to get started with minimal capital.

RETIREMENT ACCOUNTS

Real estate has long been considered a reliable way to build wealth. According to The National Association of Realtors, 90% of millionaires have some form of real estate in their portfolio.

Investing in retirement accounts like 401(k)s and IRAs is a powerful way to build wealth for the future. Contributions to these accounts are tax-advantaged, meaning you pay less tax now and can let your money grow over time.

Action Step:
Maximize contributions to your 401(k), especially if your employer offers a match. Aim to contribute at least 15% of your income to retirement accounts.

CHAPTER 5: ADVANCED WEALTH-BUILDING STRATEGIES

LEVERAGING DEBT TO BUILD WEALTH

Good Debt vs. Bad Debt: Not all debt is created equal. While high-interest consumer debt (like credit cards) is harmful to your financial health, "good" debt can actually help you grow your wealth. This includes mortgages, student loans (for income-generating skills), and business loans. According to the Federal Reserve, leveraging debt strategically can help fund investments that grow at a higher rate than the interest paid.

- <u>Using Debt for Investment</u>: For example, real estate investors often use mortgages to acquire rental properties, which generate passive income and appreciate in value over time. In the same way, using loans to fund a growing business or other income-producing ventures can accelerate wealth building.

Action Step:

If you're considering taking on debt to invest, make sure you have a solid plan for how the debt will help generate more income than it costs. Research interest rates and ensure you have a clear path to paying it off.

BUILDING MULTIPLE INCOME STREAMS

Why It's Important: Relying on a single source of income is risky. According to a report by the U.S. Bureau of Labor Statistics, 24% of workers have more than one job. Diversifying your income sources can reduce financial stress and increase your ability to save and invest.

Types of Income Streams:

- Active Income: Money earned through your job or active side hustles (e.g., freelancing, consulting).
- Passive Income: Money earned from investments or assets that require minimal effort to maintain (e.g., rental properties, dividends, royalties).
- Portfolio Income: Income earned through investments like stocks, bonds, and real estate.

Action Step:

Identify one new income stream to pursue this month, whether it's freelancing, investing in stocks, or starting a blog. Aim to increase your income by at least 25% within the next six months.

TAX OPTIMIZATION: KEEPING MORE OF WHAT YOU EARN

The Importance of Taxes: One of the most effective ways to grow wealth is by paying as little tax as legally possible. The U.S. tax code offers a variety of strategies for reducing taxable income, including retirement accounts, capital gains taxes, and tax deductions for business expenses.

Tax-Advantaged Accounts:

- 401(k)s and IRAs: Contributing to these retirement accounts lowers your taxable income for the year, while also growing your savings tax-deferred (traditional) or tax-free (Roth).
- Health Savings Accounts (HSAs): These accounts allow you to save money for medical expenses, with the triple tax benefit of contributions being tax-deductible, growing tax-free, and withdrawals for medical expenses being tax-free.

Action Step:

Max out your 401(k) and IRA contributions for the year to reduce your taxable income. If eligible, open and contribute to an HSA to boost your savings.

THE POWER OF NETWORKING AND MENTORSHIP

Why It Matters: Building relationships with others who have already achieved financial success is one of the fastest ways to learn and grow your wealth. According to a study by the Kauffman Foundation, 70% of successful entrepreneurs had mentors who helped them navigate challenges and grow their businesses.

Finding the Right Mentors: Look for people who have experience in the areas you're focusing on. This could be a successful investor, a business owner, or someone with expertise in personal finance.

Action Step:
Join networking groups (either online or in person) related to your goals. Set up informational interviews with successful individuals and ask them for advice on building wealth.

PHILANTHROPY: GIVING BACK AS YOU GROW

Why It's Part of Wealth Building: Many wealthy individuals, including Warren Buffett and Bill Gates, are committed to giving away a portion of their wealth. Philanthropy has benefits beyond helping others–it can improve your personal brand and bring a sense of purpose to your financial journey.

How to Get Started: Start small by donating to causes that matter to you. Once your wealth grows, you can consider establishing a foundation or giving back through business initiatives.

Action Step:

Identify one charitable cause to support this year. Set a goal to donate a percentage of your income (or profits) to this cause, and involve your family or friends to make it a community effort.

CHAPTER 6: MASTERING YOUR MONEY MINDSET

THE PSYCHOLOGY OF WEALTH

Mindset Shifts for Success: Your mindset plays a crucial role in how you build wealth. A fixed mindset can limit your growth, while a growth mindset opens up opportunities to learn, take risks, and succeed. According to Carol Dweck's Mindset, those who believe their abilities can be developed are more likely to thrive financially.

Overcoming Limiting Beliefs**:** Many people carry limiting beliefs about money, such as "money is hard to come by" or "rich people are selfish." These beliefs can sabotage your financial success. Replacing these with empowering beliefs, like "money is a tool to help others" and "wealth is abundant," will put you on the path to financial freedom.

Action Step:

Write down three limiting beliefs you have about money, then rewrite them as empowering beliefs. Revisit this exercise every month to reinforce your new money mindset.

THE IMPORTANCE OF FINANCIAL EDUCATION

Invest in Learning: The most successful individuals in the world are lifelong learners. Warren Buffett, for example, spends 80% of his day reading. Financial education is no different–read books, attend seminars, and listen to podcasts to continue expanding your knowledge.

Taking Action with Knowledge: Learning is only valuable if you apply it. For instance, after reading about investing in real estate, take the first step toward purchasing a property (or researching platforms to invest in REITs).

Action Step:

Commit to reading one financial book each month and setting aside 30 minutes per day to study a new wealth-building concept. Apply the knowledge to your financial journey.

CHAPTER 7: GROWING YOUR WEALTH THROUGH REAL ESTATE

THE BASICS OF REAL ESTATE INVESTMENT

Understanding the Market: Real estate is a proven way to build wealth. By owning property, you gain access to appreciation, rental income, and tax advantages. The key is understanding your market and being prepared to make informed decisions.

Types of Real Estate Investments:

- Rental Properties: Buying residential properties that generate steady rental income.
- Flipping Properties: Buying distressed properties, renovating them, and selling for a profit.
- Real Estate Investment Trusts (REITs): A more passive way to invest in real estate, as you can invest in property portfolios without owning actual property.

Action Step:

Research your local real estate market or consider online platforms for REITs. Set a goal to save for a down payment or invest in your first property within the next 12 months.

LEVERAGING REAL ESTATE FOR PASSIVE INCOME

The Power of Cash Flow: Owning rental properties can provide consistent monthly cash flow. With smart property management, rental income can cover your mortgage and generate extra profits. Over time, you can scale by acquiring more properties.

Short-Term Rentals: Platforms like Airbnb allow you to turn a property into a short-term rental, often generating higher income than traditional long-term leases.

Action Step:

If you're considering rental properties, start by saving for a down payment. If you already own property, explore how to turn it into a profitable rental on Airbnb or similar platforms.

TAX BENEFITS OF REAL ESTATE

Tax Deductions and Depreciation: Real estate investors benefit from several tax advantages, such as deductions for mortgage interest, property taxes, and depreciation. These deductions reduce your taxable income, which can help build wealth over time.

One Type of a Tax Strategy:

- 1031 Exchange: This tax strategy allows you to defer capital gains taxes when selling a property by reinvesting the proceeds into another similar property.

Action Step:

Consult with a tax professional to understand the tax benefits available to you as a real estate investor. Start tracking your property expenses to maximize your deductions.

CHAPTER 8: BUILDING WEALTH THROUGH ENTREPRENEURSHIP

THE ENTREPRENEURIAL MINDSET

Starting with a Vision: Every successful entrepreneur starts with a vision of what they want to create. Having a clear sense of purpose and direction can keep you motivated through the highs and lows of building a business.

Embracing Risk and Failure: Entrepreneurship involves risk, and failure is part of the process. Successful entrepreneurs view failure as a learning opportunity. According to Think and Grow Rich by Napoleon Hill, persistence in the face of failure is key to success.

Action Step:

Write down your business vision and the steps you need to take to bring it to life. Break down each step into manageable tasks and start taking action immediately.

BUILDING YOUR FIRST BUSINESS

Choosing the Right Business Idea: The best business ideas solve problems or fill a need in the market. Consider industries you're passionate about or areas where you have expertise. Start small and scale over time.

Funding Your Business: Many entrepreneurs start with little to no capital, bootstrapping their way to success. However, there are also options like crowdfunding, angel investors, and small business loans to consider when funding your venture.

Action Step:

Validate your business idea by conducting market research and talking to potential customers. Set a realistic goal for launching your business within the next 3-6 months.

SCALING YOUR BUSINESS

Systems and Automation: As your business grows, systems and automation become critical for efficiency. Leverage technology to streamline operations, manage customer relations, and handle finances.

Delegating and Building a Team: Successful entrepreneurs know how to delegate tasks and build a team that shares their vision. Surround yourself with people who compliment your strengths and can help scale the business.

Action Step:

Identify one area of your business that can be automated or delegated. Look into software or services that can help improve efficiency and consider hiring your first team member or freelancer.

CHAPTER 9: WEALTH PRESERVATION: PROTECTING YOUR ASSETS

UNDERSTANDING INSURANCE

The Role of Insurance in Wealth Preservation: Insurance helps protect your assets from unexpected events like accidents, illness, or property damage. Types of insurance you should consider include health insurance, life insurance, homeowners/renters insurance, and disability insurance.

- Life Insurance for Long-Term Protection: Life insurance ensures your family's financial security in case of your untimely death. Term life insurance is generally the most affordable option for most individuals.

Action Step:

Review your current insurance policies to ensure you're adequately covered. If you don't have life insurance, consider purchasing a policy to protect your family.

ESTATE PLANNING

Why You Need a Will: Estate planning is about ensuring your assets are distributed according to your wishes after you pass away. Having a will is essential to avoid confusion and potential legal battles.

Trusts and Tax Strategies: If your wealth grows significantly, setting up a trust can help reduce estate taxes and ensure your assets go to your heirs without unnecessary complications.

Action Step:

Consult with an estate planning attorney to create a will or trust that aligns with your goals. Make sure your beneficiaries are up to date on all accounts and investments.

DIVERSIFICATION TO PROTECT WEALTH

Spreading Risk Across Asset Classes: Diversifying your investments–across stocks, bonds, real estate, and even alternative investments–helps protect your wealth from volatility. The more diversified your portfolio, the less risk you're exposed to in the event of market downturns.

Action Step:

Review your investment portfolio to ensure it's diversified. Aim to invest in different asset classes and industries to reduce risk and build a stable wealth foundation.

CHAPTER 10: THE POWER OF PASSIVE INCOME

WHAT IS PASSIVE INCOME?

Definition and Benefits: Passive income is money earned with minimal effort or active involvement. Unlike active income (where you trade time for money), passive income allows you to earn money while you sleep, giving you the freedom to work on other projects or enjoy life.

Common Passive Income Streams:

- Dividends from Stocks: Earning dividends from investments in companies that pay regular payouts to shareholders.
- Royalties: From writing books, creating music, or inventing products.
- Automated Online Businesses: Building e-commerce stores, digital product sales, or membership sites.
- Rental Income: As mentioned before, rental properties are a source of passive income.

Action Step:

Choose one passive income stream to focus on in the next 6 months. Create a plan to get started, whether that's investing in dividend stocks or setting up an online store.

BUILDING SYSTEMS FOR PASSIVE INCOME

Automation and Outsourcing: The key to creating truly passive income is automation. Setting up systems and outsourcing tasks allows the income stream to run on autopilot. For example, if you sell digital products, you can use platforms like Gumroad or Shopify to handle transactions automatically.

Building a Content Library: If you're interested in creating passive income through content (e-books, online courses, or blogs), the best approach is to create a library of content that continues to attract people over time. This can generate income for years to come.

Action Step:

Identify one area of your life where you can implement automation (e.g., automated email marketing, an online course that generates income). Start by setting up the automation tools needed for success.

CHAPTER 11: WEALTH BUILDING THROUGH DIGITAL PRODUCTS AND ONLINE BUSINESSES

CREATING AND SELLING DIGITAL PRODUCTS

What Are Digital Products?: These are products that can be delivered electronically, such as e-books, courses, software, music, or a printable. They are highly scalable because you can sell them to an unlimited number of people once the product is created.

How to Create Your Own Digital Product: Think about problems people face and how you can solve them. For instance, a beginner-level online course teaching personal finance or a toolkit for aspiring entrepreneurs could provide value and generate income.

Action Step:

Brainstorm ideas for a digital product you can create. Start with an outline and aim to create a minimum viable product (MVP) within the next 3 months.

BUILDING AN ONLINE BUSINESS

Choosing the Right Online Business Model: There are multiple types of online business models, including e-commerce, affiliate marketing, subscription-based services, and coaching. Each has its own pros and cons, so it's important to choose the one that aligns with your skills and goals.

E-commerce and Dropshipping: E-commerce businesses allow you to sell physical products online. Dropshipping, in particular, allows you to sell products without holding inventory–your supplier handles storage and shipping.

Action Step:

Research different online business models and select one to pursue. Begin with a small-scale version of the business and test the market before scaling.

MARKETING YOUR DIGITAL PRODUCTS

Using Social Media to Drive Sales: Social media platforms like Instagram, TikTok, and YouTube are great tools to promote your digital products. They allow you to build a following and engage with potential customers directly.

Email Marketing and Automation: Building an email list is one of the most effective ways to market digital products. Automated email sequences can nurture leads and convert them into paying customers.

Action Step:

Start building your email list and create an automated email sequence that introduces your digital product to subscribers. Use social media to attract people to your email list.

CHAPTER 12: THE POWER OF FINANCIAL EDUCATION AND CONTINUOUS LEARNING

WHY FINANCIAL EDUCATION IS KEY

Financial education equips you with the knowledge to make informed decisions, avoid common financial pitfalls, and maximize wealth-building strategies. Whether it's learning about new investment opportunities, tax laws, or economic trends, ongoing education is essential.

Ways to Develop Financial Education:

- Read Books and Articles: Financial literacy books like Rich Dad Poor Dad by Robert Kiyosaki or The Intelligent Investor by Benjamin Graham offer timeless advice.
- Take Courses and Attend Seminars: Online platforms like Coursera, Udemy, and even local workshops can provide valuable insights into money management and investment strategies.
- Follow Thought Leaders: Stay updated with blogs, podcasts, or YouTube channels run by financial experts. They often share the latest trends and opportunities.

Action Step:

Dedicate 30 minutes a day to learning something new about finance. Choose a course or a book and set a timeline to finish it.

TAKE ONLINE COURSES AND ATTEND WORKSHOPS

Formal education rarely teaches personal finance, but today, there are endless online resources to bridge the gap.

Where to Learn:

- Coursera & Udemy: Offer finance and investing courses from experts.
- YouTube Channels: Creators like Graham Stephan and Andrei Jikh break down personal finance in simple terms.
- Financial Podcasts; Shows like The Dave Ramsey Show or BiggerPockets Money provide real-world money advice.
- Local Workshops: Many banks and financial institutions offer free financial literacy classes.

Action Step:

Enroll in a free online finance course or attend a workshop within the next week. Take notes on key lessons learned.

FOLLOW THOUGHT LEADERS AND EXPERTS

Staying updated on the latest financial trends and strategies is crucial. Wealthy individuals constantly follow expert advice and industry news.

Who to Follow:

- Warren Buffett (Investing): Follow his shareholder letters and investment insights.
- Ramit Sethi (Personal Finance): Author of I Will Teach You to Be Rich, shares practical money tips.
- Tasha Cochran (One Big Happy Life): Focuses on financial independence and wealth-building for families.

Action Step:

Subscribe to a financial expert's newsletter, YouTube channel, or podcast and commit to consuming at least one piece of content weekly.

JOIN FINANCIAL COMMUNITIES AND NETWORKING GROUPS

Surrounding yourself with like-minded individuals can accelerate your learning and keep you motivated. Many successful people attribute their financial growth to networking and mentorship.

Where to Connect:

- Reddit Communities: r/financialindependence, r/personalfinance
- Facebook Groups: Personal finance and investment groups
- Local Meetups: Join entrepreneurship and finance-related events in your city
- Mastermind Groups: Many successful entrepreneurs form groups to exchange financial strategies

Action Step:

Join an online finance community today. Engage in at least one discussion this week.

LEARN ABOUT TAXES AND LEGAL STRATEGIES

Understanding tax laws can save you thousands of dollars every year. The wealthy use legal tax strategies to protect and grow their wealth.

Tax-Saving Strategies:

- Tax-Advantaged Accounts: Use 401(k)s, IRAs, and HSAs to reduce taxable income.
- Capital Gains Optimization: Hold investments longer to qualify for lower tax rates.
- Business Tax Deductions: Entrepreneurs can write off business expenses like travel, meals, and home office costs.

Action Step:

Research one tax strategy you can apply to your financial situation.

CHAPTER 13: BUILDING WEALTH THROUGH STOCK MARKET STRATEGIES

STOCK MARKET BASICS

Understanding the stock market can be a powerful tool in building wealth. Whether you're a long-term investor or interested in trading, the stock market offers a variety of opportunities for wealth growth.

Types of Stocks to Look Into:

- Investing in Index Funds: Low-cost index funds allow you to invest in the broader market and diversify your portfolio.
- Dividend Investing: Dividend stocks provide regular payouts, which can be reinvested for compound growth.
- Growth vs. Value Stocks: Understand the difference between growth stocks (high potential for growth but more risk) and value stocks (stable, undervalued stocks).

Action Step:

Choose one stock market investment strategy (index funds, dividend investing, or growth vs. value stocks) and research three potential investments that align with it. Write down why each investment interests you and track its performance over the next month.

ACTIVE VS. PASSIVE INVESTING

The Difference Between Active & Passive:

- Active Investing: Requires more time and effort to research and pick individual stocks.
- Passive Investing: Focuses on buying and holding low-cost index funds, requiring less time and attention but still providing significant returns over the long term.

Action Step:

Open a brokerage account and start by investing in an index fund or stock that aligns with your financial goals.

CHAPTER 14: TURNING YOUR PASSION INTO PROFIT

IDENTIFYING YOUR PASSION

Passion-driven businesses can be more fulfilling and profitable. By focusing on something you genuinely care about, you can sustain motivation and overcome challenges more easily.

How to Identify Your Passion:

- Finding Your Niche: Think about what excites you, whether it's a hobby, a talent, or a cause. The more specific your niche, the better.
- Market Research: Even if you love your passion, research whether there's demand for it. Look for trends, competitors, and potential customers.

Action Step:

Write down three passions or interests that excite you. Then, research each one to identify potential business opportunities by analyzing market demand, competitors, and audience needs. Choose the most viable option and outline a basic plan to turn it into a profitable venture.

CREATING INCOME STREAMS AROUND YOUR PASSION

Once you've identified your passion, here's how you can turn it into income:

Types of Income Streams to Start:

- Create an Online Course: Share your expertise in a particular subject and sell your knowledge.
- Start a Blog, YouTube Channel, or Podcast: Monetize your platform with ads, sponsorships, or affiliate marketing.
- Sell Products or Merchandise: Whether it's handmade goods, digital products, or branded items, there are many ways to monetize your creativity.

Action Step:

Identify one way to monetize your passion. Create a plan to launch your first income stream related to it.

CHAPTER 15: CREATING MULTIPLE STREAMS OF INCOME

WHY MULTIPLE INCOME STREAMS MATTER

Relying on a single income stream is risky. By diversifying your sources of income, you can protect yourself against economic downturns and increase your overall earning potential.

Different Streams of Income:

- Earned Income: Your salary or wages from a job or business.
- Investment Income: Earnings from dividends, interest, or capital gains.
- Passive Income: Income that requires minimal effort after the initial setup, such as from rental properties, royalties, or digital products.

Action Step:

Assess your current income streams and identify at least one new income source to develop. Start by researching an investment opportunity, a side hustle, or a passive income idea that aligns with your skills and financial goals. Set a timeline to take the first step toward implementing it.

HOW TO BUILD MULTIPLE STREAMS

Relying on just one source of income can limit your financial growth and put you at risk if that income disappears. Successful wealth builders create multiple streams of income to ensure financial stability and long-term wealth. By leveraging your existing skills, taking advantage of technology, and making smart investments, you can build additional revenue sources that complement your main income. Whether it's starting a side hustle, investing in real estate, or monetizing your expertise online, diversifying your income is a key step toward financial freedom.

Tips on How to Build Multiple Streams:

- Start with What You Know: Use your existing skills and knowledge to create additional income streams.
- Leverage Technology: Use online platforms like Etsy, Patreon, or Udemy to create scalable income streams.
- Invest in Real Estate: If you're new to investing, consider starting with rental properties or REITs to create a source of passive income.

Action Step:

Brainstorm three ways you can create additional income streams this year. Pick one to start and make a plan to launch it.

CHAPTER 16: MASTERING HIGH-INCOME SKILLS FOR FINANCIAL GROWTH

WHY HIGH-INCOME SKILLS MATTER

High-income skills are crucial for increasing your earning potential and achieving financial independence. These skills give you the flexibility to earn based on your expertise and can be the difference between a steady salary and significant financial growth. The more valuable your skill, the more you can command in terms of pay or business success.

Types of High-Income Skills:

- Sales & Persuasion: Mastering the ability to sell–whether it's a product, service, or idea–can open endless income opportunities.
- Copywriting & Digital Marketing: Businesses constantly need skilled marketers to drive sales and brand growth.
- Coding & Tech Skills: Software development, AI expertise, and data analysis are among the most in-demand skills today.

Action Step:

Identify a high-income skill that aligns with your strengths or interests. Spend 30 minutes daily to start learning or improving it, either through courses, books, or tutorials.

HOW TO MONETIZE YOUR HIGH-INCOME SKILLS

Once you've developed a high-income skill, it's time to explore ways to monetize it. Freelancing and consulting are immediate options where you can offer your expertise on platforms like Upwork or LinkedIn. Additionally, teaching or coaching others through online courses can also turn your skill into a profitable income stream.

Tips on How to Build Multiple Streams:

- <u>Freelancing & Consulting:</u> Offer your expertise on platforms like Upwork, Fiverr, and LinkedIn.
- <u>Building a Business:</u> Turn your skill into a full-fledged service or product-based business.
- <u>Teaching & Coaching:</u> Monetize your knowledge through online courses, coaching programs, or memberships.

Action Step:

Create a list of ways to monetize your skill, and choose one to start with. Whether it's offering a service or creating a course, take the first step today.

ACTION STEP & IMPLEMENTATION

Learning a high-income skill is just the beginning. To successfully monetize it, you need a clear plan and action steps. By creating a portfolio, offering your services to potential clients, and continuously improving your skills, you can turn your expertise into a profitable venture.

How to Take Action & Implement

- Choose One Skill: Pick a high-income skill based on your strengths and interests.
- Dedicate Learning Time: Set aside at least 30 minutes daily to improve your chosen skill.
- Start Small: Offer your services for free or at a discounted rate to gain experience.
- Create a Portfolio: Showcase your work through case studies, testimonials, or samples.
- Monetize It: Apply for jobs, offer freelance services, or create a business around your skill.

Action Step:

Develop a portfolio showcasing your skill. Reach out to potential clients, offering your services for free or at a discounted rate to build experience.

CHAPTER 17: WEALTH BUILDING THROUGH FRUGALITY AND SMART SPENDING

WHY FRUGALITY ACCELERATES WEALTH

Building wealth isn't just about making more money; it's about managing and keeping the money you earn. Smart spending habits, like budgeting and prioritizing savings, can accelerate your wealth-building journey. When you control your expenses, you can invest more into wealth-building opportunities.

Tips on How to Build Multiple Streams:

- The Power of Budgeting: Understanding where your money goes helps maximize savings and investments.
- The 50/30/20 Rule: Allocate income efficiently–50% needs, 30% wants, 20% savings/investments.
- Minimalism & Intentional Spending: Buy what truly adds value to your life instead of excessive consumption.

Action Step:

Review your current spending habits for the past month. Track where your money goes and identify areas where you can cut back to save more.

SMART SPENDING STRATEGIES FOR LONG-TERM WEALTH

Cutting unnecessary expenses can lead to significant wealth growth over time. Strategies like negotiating bills, taking advantage of cashback rewards, and making intentional purchases can free up more money for investments. It's important to consider the long-term impact of your spending decisions, rather than focusing on short-term gratification.

How to Take Action & Implement

- Negotiating Bills & Expenses: Lower costs on insurance, subscriptions, and services.
- Cashback & Reward Programs: Leverage credit card rewards and loyalty programs for extra savings.
- The Buy-and-Hold Mentality: Invest in high-quality items instead of constantly repurchasing cheap alternatives.

Action Step:

Identify at least three monthly expenses that can be reduced. Cancel subscriptions, switch to cheaper services, or negotiate your bills for better rates.

ACTION PLAN & EXECUTION

Cutting unnecessary expenses can lead to significant wealth growth over time. Strategies like negotiating bills, taking advantage of cashback rewards, and making intentional purchases can free up more money for investments. It's important to consider the long-term impact of your spending decisions, rather than focusing on short-term gratification.

How to Take Action & Implement

- Track Your Expenses: Review your spending habits over the past three months.
- Identify Unnecessary Costs: Cancel unused subscriptions or find lower-cost alternatives.
- Optimize Your Budget: Adjust your spending to save at least 10-20% more each month.
- Find Cost-Saving Hacks: Use cashback apps, negotiate bills, and buy in bulk when possible.
- Redirect Savings to Investments: Use the money saved to invest in income-generating assets.

Action Step:

Audit your spending for the past three months. Identify unnecessary expenses and set a goal to redirect those funds toward savings or investments.

CHAPTER 18: LEVERAGING AUTOMATION FOR WEALTH GROWTH

WHY AUTOMATION IS KEY TO FINANCIAL SUCCESS

Automation is a game-changer when it comes to managing your finances and business. By automating key tasks such as savings, investments, and bill payments, you eliminate the chance of human error and reduce the mental load of financial management. It also allows you to focus on wealth-building activities that require your direct attention.

- Set It and Forget It: Automated systems remove human error and ensure financial consistency.
- Consistency in Investing & Saving: Automated transfers make wealth accumulation effortless.
- Scalability in Business: Business automation allows you to earn more while working less.

Action Step:

Set up one automated financial process this week, such as automatic savings or bill payments, to save time and ensure consistency.

FINANCIAL & BUSINESS AUTOMATION STRATEGIES

Automating your finances can free up time to focus on income-generating activities. You can set up automatic transfers into savings or investment accounts, schedule bill payments to avoid late fees, and streamline business operations through software tools. These systems reduce stress and make your wealth-building efforts more efficient.

- Automatic Savings & Investments: Set up direct deposits into savings and investment accounts.
- Automated Bill Payments: Avoid late fees by scheduling payments for credit cards, utilities, and loans.
- Passive Income Through Automation: Use AI chatbots, auto-responders, and content scheduling tools to streamline business operations.

Action Step:

Set up one automated financial process this week, such as automatic savings or bill payments, to save time and ensure consistency.

CHAPTER 19: MASTERING THE ART OF NEGOTIATION FOR FINANCIAL SUCCESS

WHY NEGOTIATION SKILLS MATTER

Negotiation is an essential skill that can increase your income, reduce your expenses, and help you secure better deals. Whether you're negotiating a salary, business contract, or investment terms, being able to negotiate effectively can save or earn you significant amounts of money. Mastering this skill is crucial for financial success and wealth accumulation.

- Boost Your Earnings: Negotiating salaries, freelance rates, or business contracts can significantly increase income.
- Cut Costs: Lower bills, rent, and service expenses through skillful negotiation.
- Gain Leverage in Deals: The right negotiation tactics can help you get better terms in investments or business deals.

Action Step:

Find one area of your life where you can apply negotiation skills. Whether it's negotiating your salary, a business deal, or a bill, take the first step today.

EFFECTIVE NEGOTIATION STRATEGIES

To maximize your negotiating power, use these proven strategies: research beforehand, start high, and use silence to create pressure. Understanding the other party's interests and building rapport also ensures better outcomes. Negotiation is not just about getting the best deal but also about creating value for both sides.

- Do Your Research: Understand market rates, competitors, and financial factors before entering a negotiation.
- Start High, Then Adjust: Always ask for more than you expect, giving room for compromise.
- Use Silence as a Tool: Allow pauses to create pressure on the other party to offer better terms.
- Build Rapport: Establishing a good relationship can lead to better negotiation outcomes.

Action Step:

Find one area of your life where you can apply negotiation skills. Whether it's negotiating your salary, a business deal, or a bill, take the first step today.

CHAPTER 20: BUILDING WEALTH THROUGH CROWDFUNDING AND PEER-TO-PEER INVESTMENTS

UNDERSTANDING CROWDFUNDING AS AN INVESTMENT OPPORTUNITY

Crowdfunding platforms have allowed small investors to access opportunities that were once available only to large institutions. According to a 2019 study by the National Bureau of Economic Research, crowdfunding platforms like Kickstarter and Fundrise have democratized access to real estate investments and startup funding, with returns outperforming some traditional asset classes in certain cases. The growth in the crowdfunding space suggests that, for some investors, this could be a viable strategy to diversify portfolios and accelerate wealth-building. Fundrise, a popular real estate crowdfunding platform, has helped over 130,000 investors with a 9.47% annual return on average over the last 5 years.

Actionable Steps for Crowdfunding Investments

- Research Different Platforms: Explore crowdfunding platforms like Fundrise, SeedInvest, or RealtyMogul to understand the types of investments available.
- Assess Each Investment's Potential: Focus on businesses or projects with a strong foundation, clear business models, and experienced leadership.
- Start with Low Investment Amounts: To mitigate risks, start with small investments to build experience before scaling up.

Action Step:

Select one crowdfunding platform, sign up, and make an investment in a project that interests you. Track your investment's progress regularly.

MANAGING RISK IN CROWDFUNDING INVESTMENTS

Crowdfunding comes with risks, but studies show that diversifying your investments can significantly mitigate these risks. A study by Harvard Business School found that angel investors who spread their investments across multiple startups had a much higher likelihood of seeing a profitable return. In fact, a diversified portfolio can reduce the chance of total loss by helping to balance high-risk investments with more stable opportunities. A Harvard study showed that for every 1 in 10 angel investments that fails, 2-3 provide a substantial return. Diversifying across 20 startups could mean that 2-3 succeed in a way that makes up for the rest.

Investment Risk Management Strategies

- Diversify Your Portfolio: Spread your investments across multiple projects to avoid putting all your capital into one.
- Research and Due Diligence: Read the business plan, financials, and updates from the companies you're investing in to understand the risks involved.
- Monitor Your Investments: Regularly check the status of your investments and stay informed about the project's performance and challenges.

Action Step:

Diversify your portfolio by investing in different crowdfunding projects with varying risk profiles. Set a reminder to track the performance of each project monthly.

GROWING YOUR WEALTH THROUGH CROWDFUNDING

Research from McKinsey & Company highlights that reinvesting your returns into crowdfunding opportunities can accelerate wealth growth. Investors who reinvest profits regularly into high-growth sectors, like technology and clean energy, have seen significant compounded returns over a 5-10 year period. By staying informed and tracking trends, you can make smarter investment decisions that align with market opportunities. According to McKinsey, early investors in the green energy sector (like those using crowdfunding platforms) saw their investment grow by 400% between 2010 and 2018.

Strategies for Scaling Your Crowdfunding Investments

- Reinvest Earnings: Use returns from successful investments to fund new projects and increase your exposure to growing sectors.
- Follow Trends: Stay updated on industry trends and new investment opportunities in emerging markets.
- Evaluate New Opportunities Regularly: Continually assess new crowdfunding campaigns and choose those with the best growth potential.

Action Step:

Reinvest at least 50% of any returns from your crowdfunding investments into new projects. Monitor crowdfunding trends to stay ahead of the curve.

CHAPTER 21: BUILDING WEALTH THROUGH FRANCHISING

WHY FRANCHISING CAN BE A PATH TO WEALTH

Franchising has long been recognized as a stable wealth-building model, with data showing that it can outperform many other small businesses. According to the International Franchise Association (IFA), the franchise industry contributed $770 billion to the U.S. economy in 2019, with franchises accounting for 3% of all businesses. The franchising model provides a proven framework for business growth, which can minimize the risks of starting a new venture from scratch.

Why Franchising Works as a Wealth-Building Tool:

- Established Brand: The franchise brand already has recognition, reducing the time it takes to build your customer base.
- Proven Systems: Franchisors offer established operational systems and marketing strategies, which increase the chances of success.
- Support Network: With a franchise, you receive ongoing support, training, and resources to help you grow your business.

Action Step:

Research franchise opportunities that match your skills and interests. Make a list of 3 franchises you're interested in and evaluate their investment requirements.

FINANCING YOUR FRANCHISE BUSINESS

Financing a franchise requires careful planning and an understanding of your options. Research by the U.S. Small Business Administration (SBA) shows that 25% of small business loans are directed toward franchises, and those loans have a higher rate of success than other small businesses. According to SBA data, franchises are less likely to default on loans due to the brand's established reputation and operational support.

Key Considerations for Financing a Franchise:

- Understand the Total Costs: Assess the initial investment and ongoing fees, including royalties and marketing contributions.
- Explore Financing Options: Many banks offer loans for franchise businesses, and some franchisors assist with financing options.
- Seek SBA Loans: The U.S. Small Business Administration (SBA) offers loan programs tailored for franchise businesses.

Action Step:

Calculate the initial costs of a franchise you're interested in, and research potential financing options, including SBA loans or bank financing.

MANAGING AND SCALING YOUR FRANCHISE BUSINESS

Studies show that the key to successful scaling in franchising is systemization and consistency. Deloitte found that franchises that maintain a consistent customer experience across multiple locations grow at a 35% faster rate than those that do not standardize their operations. Scaling through operational efficiency and maintaining brand consistency is critical to long-term franchise success.

Strategies for Growing Your Franchise

- Optimize Operations: Streamline daily operations, including employee management and supply chain logistics, to reduce costs and increase efficiency.
- Customer Retention: Focus on creating a loyal customer base through exceptional service and effective marketing.
- Expansion: Consider opening additional locations or buying into other franchise opportunities once your first franchise is profitable.

Action Step:

Create a growth plan for your franchise, detailing steps for optimizing operations, retaining customers, and expanding into new locations.

CHAPTER 22: BUILDING WEALTH THROUGH ANGEL INVESTING

THE BASICS OF ANGEL INVESTING

Angel investing is known for its high returns, but it comes with higher risks as well. A study from University of California, Berkeley found that angel investors who carefully select startups can see returns of 2.6 times their original investment over a period of 4-5 years. Angel investing isn't for everyone, but it offers an attractive opportunity for those with a strong risk tolerance.

How to Get Started with Angel Investing:

- Identify Promising Startups: Look for innovative startups in emerging industries or those solving significant problems.
- Conduct Due Diligence: Assess the startup's business model, leadership team, and market opportunity before investing.
- Understand the Risks: Be prepared for the possibility that many startups may fail, and invest only what you can afford to lose.

Action Step:

Research angel investment platforms like AngelList or SeedInvest, and create a list of startups that align with your investment goals. Start with small investments to build experience.

EVALUATING STARTUPS FOR ANGEL INVESTING

To mitigate risks, conducting due diligence is critical in the angel investing process. A study by Harvard Business Review found that investors who took the time to thoroughly vet companies, including the leadership team and market conditions, were 50% more likely to make a successful investment. It's not just about the idea, but about the execution and the team behind it.

How to Evaluate Startups for Angel Investing:

- Research the Founders and Leadership Team: Investigate the backgrounds of the leadership team. A strong, experienced team can often make up for a less-than-perfect idea.
- Examine the Business Model: Understand how the startup plans to make money, who its target market is, and how it plans to scale. A solid and scalable business model is crucial for long-term success.
- Analyze Market Conditions and Competition: Evaluate the market size and competition. A great idea is only successful if it addresses a real problem in a growing market with manageable competition.

Action Step:

To assess a startup's potential, research the leadership team's background and past experiences, focusing on their ability to execute and grow the business. Review the company's pitch deck, business model, and market trends to ensure it addresses a relevant gap and has scalable potential.

CHAPTER 23: MASTERING REAL ESTATE FLIPPING FOR PROFIT

WHY REAL ESTATE FLIPPING IS A LUCRATIVE INVESTMENT

Flipping real estate can be a highly profitable investment strategy if approached correctly. The ability to purchase undervalued properties, renovate them, and sell them at a higher price point is one of the most well-known ways to generate significant returns. Success in this space requires a keen eye for opportunity, market knowledge, and the ability to manage renovation projects efficiently.

Key Considerations for a Successful Flip:

- Location is Key: Choose areas with a high demand for homes, and research the neighborhood's growth potential. Target locations with rising property values to maximize your return.
- Understand Property Values: Ensure that the property you purchase is below market value, but don't overestimate how much you can sell it for after renovations. Know what buyers are looking for.
- Renovate Wisely: Focus on improvements that add the most value to the property, like kitchen upgrades, new flooring, or bathroom remodels. Keep your budget in check to avoid costly over-improvements.

Action Step:

Research local real estate markets to identify three properties that could be purchased for a low price, renovated, and sold for a profit. Set up a meeting with a local realtor to better understand the market dynamics.

HOW TO ANALYZE A PROPERTY FOR FLIPPING

Before diving into real estate flipping, it's critical to evaluate whether the investment is worth the time and money. Understanding both the cost of renovation and the potential resale value is essential for minimizing risk. Perform thorough due diligence and calculate the expected profit margin before purchasing any property.

Evaluating a Potential Property for Flipping

- Inspect the Property: Assess the property's foundation, structure, plumbing, electrical system, and roofing. If major issues are uncovered, they can quickly eat into your profit.
- Estimate Renovation Costs: Get multiple contractor quotes and estimate the timeline for repairs. Make sure to leave room in your budget for unexpected issues that may arise.
- Analyze Comparable Sales: Research similar properties in the area that have recently sold, focusing on their price after renovations. This will give you a realistic expectation of the resale price.

Action Step:

Choose a property you're considering flipping, and calculate the renovation cost and expected resale value. Use online tools and local market data to estimate potential profits, ensuring there's a healthy margin.

ACTION STEP & IMPLEMENTATION FOR REAL ESTATE FLIPPING

Executing a successful flip involves a well-thought-out plan and careful management of resources. By taking action, keeping costs under control, and staying on top of the project, you can turn a dilapidated property into a highly profitable asset. The key is to be proactive and prepared for the unexpected.

Steps to Manage and Complete Your Flip:

- Create a Project Timeline: Set clear milestones for each phase of the renovation. Hold contractors accountable to stay on schedule.
- Stay Within Budget: Regularly track your renovation expenses and adjust as needed. It's easy to overspend, so staying disciplined is crucial.
- Market the Property Effectively: Once renovations are complete, market the property aggressively using both traditional and online methods. Hold open houses and leverage online real estate platforms to attract buyers.

Action Step:

Develop a timeline for your property flip, setting specific deadlines for each phase of the renovation. Track your expenses regularly to ensure you stay on budget, and market the property once completed.

CHAPTER 24: BUILDING A HIGH-VALUE PERSONAL BRAND FOR WEALTH

WHY A STRONG PERSONAL BRAND IS ESSENTIAL

In today's world, your personal brand is one of your most valuable assets. A strong, recognizable brand can open doors to new opportunities, partnerships, and even revenue streams. By positioning yourself as an expert in your field, you can attract the right audience and monetize your skills.

Core Elements of a Powerful Personal Brand:

- Be Authentic: Show your true self, share your values, and be consistent in how you present yourself. Authenticity creates trust and builds deeper connections with your audience.
- Leverage Social Media: Social platforms like Instagram, LinkedIn, and TikTok allow you to showcase your expertise and build a dedicated following. Engage with your audience to increase visibility.
- Provide Value: Consistently offer helpful information, services, or insights to your audience. The more value you provide, the more likely people are to follow and engage with your brand.

Action Step:

Choose one social media platform to focus on for your personal brand. Post valuable content consistently and engage with your audience daily to start building a following.

HOW TO MONETIZE YOUR PERSONAL BRAND

Once you've established your personal brand, it's time to monetize it. There are numerous ways to turn your influence into income, from offering paid services to selling digital products. Building a sustainable income stream from your personal brand requires strategic planning and audience engagement.

Ways to Turn Your Brand into Income:

- Offer Consulting or Coaching: Use your expertise to provide one-on-one or group coaching sessions. Leverage platforms like Zoom or Skype to reach clients.
- Create Digital Products: Sell e-books, online courses, or downloadable resources. Your audience is often eager to learn more from you and will be willing to pay for valuable content.
- Partner with Brands: Seek brand partnerships or sponsorships in your niche. Collaborating with brands can provide a steady income stream while boosting your credibility.

Action Step:

Identify two ways to monetize your personal brand (coaching, courses, or products). Start by creating a simple online course or offering consulting services to your audience.

ACTION STEP & IMPLEMENTATION FOR BUILDING YOUR BRAND

To successfully build and monetize your personal brand, it's essential to take consistent action. This involves not only creating content but also engaging with your audience and providing value. Over time, your brand will evolve, and your income opportunities will increase.

Effective Strategies for Brand Growth:

- Create a Content Plan: Develop a strategy for regular content creation across platforms. Set clear goals for audience growth and engagement.
- Engage with Your Audience: Respond to comments, ask for feedback, and build a loyal community. The more you engage, the stronger your connection will be.
- Collaborate with Other Influencers: Partner with others in your industry to cross-promote each other's brands. This can help you expand your reach and credibility.

Action Step:

Set a goal to post valuable content three times a week for the next month. Engage with your audience by responding to comments and asking for feedback on your posts.

CHAPTER 25: BUILDING WEALTH THROUGH INTELLECTUAL PROPERTY

WHY INTELLECTUAL PROPERTY IS A LUCRATIVE ASSET

Intellectual property (IP) is one of the most undervalued yet highly lucrative assets for wealth building. From patents to copyrights, your intellectual property can generate consistent passive income, whether through licensing, royalties, or sales. The key is to protect and leverage your creations to maximize their potential.

Key Strategies for Monetizing IP:

- Patent Your Inventions: If you have created something unique, securing a patent protects your idea and allows you to profit from it.
- Copyright Your Work: Copyrighting books, art, music, or software gives you the exclusive right to distribute and profit from your creations.
- Trademark Your Brand: Trademarks protect your brand name, logo, and slogan, ensuring no one else can profit from your intellectual property.

Action Step:

Research how to patent, copyright, or trademark your ideas. Begin the process of registering your intellectual property to protect and leverage it for future income.

HOW TO MONETIZE YOUR INTELLECTUAL PROPERTY

Once you've secured your intellectual property, there are several ways to generate revenue from it. Licensing your patents, selling your artwork, or collecting royalties from music or books can provide you with a steady income stream. The key is to actively market and distribute your IP to reach a broad audience.

Monetization Methods for Your IP

- Licensing: Allow others to use your intellectual property in exchange for a royalty or licensing fee.
- Selling Rights: If you don't want to manage the IP yourself, selling the rights can provide a lump sum payout.
- Create Multiple Products: Use your IP as the foundation for creating multiple related products that you can sell or license.

Action Step:

Identify one piece of intellectual property you own and explore ways to monetize it. Consider licensing or selling the rights to generate passive income.

TAKING ACTION FOR INTELLECTUAL PROPERTY MONETIZATION

Successfully monetizing intellectual property requires you to market and protect your creations strategically. Whether you're licensing your work or selling it, the goal is to establish long-term income streams. By understanding the market demand for your IP, you can maximize its value.

Effective Strategies for Monetizing Your IP:

- Market Your IP: Use online platforms or business partnerships to market your creations. Websites like Etsy, Amazon, or Patreon can help you distribute your work to a wider audience.
- Track Revenue: Monitor how much income your intellectual property generates, and keep track of licensing or royalty payments.
- Expand Your Portfolio: Continue to create new IP and build a portfolio that can generate multiple income streams.

Action Step:

Set up an online platform to showcase your intellectual property. Start monetizing by offering it for sale or licensing to interested buyers.

CHAPTER 26: THE SCIENCE OF WEALTH ACCUMULATION: WHAT RESEARCH SAYS

THE PSYCHOLOGY OF WEALTH AND FINANCIAL SUCCESS

Building wealth isn't just about making money–it's about understanding the mindset and habits that lead to financial success. Research from Stanford University on delayed gratification (the famous "Marshmallow Experiment") found that people who practiced self-discipline and patience were more likely to achieve long-term success, including financial stability. Wealthy individuals often have a growth mindset, continuously seeking knowledge and new opportunities.

Key Psychological Traits of Wealthy Individuals:

- Delayed Gratification: The ability to wait for bigger rewards rather than seeking instant gratification.
- Financial Confidence: A belief in one's ability to make smart money decisions and investments.
- Resilience: The ability to bounce back from financial setbacks without losing focus on long-term goals.

Action Step:

Identify one area of your finances where you struggle with delayed gratification. Set a challenge for yourself to wait longer before making unnecessary purchases.

THE HABITS OF SELF-MADE MILLIONAIRES

Thomas Corley, author of Rich Habits: The Daily Success Habits of Wealthy Individuals, spent five years studying the daily routines of self-made millionaires. His research found that 88% of wealthy people read for self-improvement, 76% exercise regularly, and 67% limit their TV time to less than an hour a day. These habits separate financially successful individuals from the average person.

Common Habits of Wealthy People:

- Lifelong Learning: Many self-made millionaires dedicate time to reading and expanding their knowledge.
- Intentional Goal-Setting: They create specific financial and personal development goals and track their progress.
- Networking with the Right People: They surround themselves with successful, motivated individuals who encourage growth.

Action Step:

Choose one new habit from this list to adopt for the next 30 days. Track your progress and note any changes in your mindset or financial situation.

LESSONS FROM REAL-LIFE WEALTH BUILDERS

Many of today's billionaires and financial success stories didn't start rich–they followed key strategies to grow their wealth over time. For example, Warren Buffett began investing at age 11 and emphasizes the importance of patience and compound interest. Another example is Barbara Corcoran, who turned a $1,000 loan into a $66 million real estate empire through strategic investments and marketing.

Real-Life Wealth-Building Examples:

- Warren Buffett: Advocates for long-term investing and avoiding emotional decisions in the stock market.
- Barbara Corcoran: Built her fortune by recognizing market trends and leveraging her personal brand.
- Chris Hogan: A former debt-ridden individual who became a personal finance expert, teaching others how to achieve financial independence.

Action Step:

Research one successful entrepreneur or investor who started with little and grew their wealth. Write down three lessons from their journey that you can apply to your own financial goals.

CHAPTER 27: MASTERING HIGH-STAKES DECISION-MAKING FOR FINANCIAL GROWTH

WHY DECISION-MAKING IS CRITICAL FOR WEALTH

Every financial decision you make, big or small, impacts your long-term wealth. The ability to make high-stakes decisions with confidence can be the difference between success and failure. Learning to evaluate risks, opportunities, and potential outcomes is key to financial growth.

Core Principles of Smart Decision-Making:

- Use Data, Not Emotion: Make decisions based on logic, research, and historical trends rather than impulse or fear.
- Weigh Risks vs. Rewards: Consider both the potential upside and downside before committing to a financial move.
- Seek Expert Advice: Consult with professionals or mentors to gain different perspectives before making major decisions.

Action Step:

Identify one major financial decision you need to make. List out the risks and rewards, then research expert opinions before finalizing your choice.

HOW TO IMPROVE YOUR FINANCIAL DECISION-MAKING

Many people struggle with decision-making due to fear of failure. The most successful individuals recognize that not every decision will be perfect, but the ability to adapt and learn from mistakes is crucial. The more informed your choices, the higher your chances of success.

Techniques to Improve Decision-Making

- Set Clear Financial Goals: When you have defined objectives, making decisions becomes easier because you know what aligns with your vision.
- Use the 10-10-10 Rule: Ask yourself–how will this decision affect me in 10 minutes, 10 months, and 10 years?
- Embrace Calculated Risks: Some of the biggest financial wins come from well-researched risks rather than playing it safe.

Action Step:

The next time you're faced with a financial decision, apply the 10-10-10 rule to assess its long-term impact before making a choice.

AVOIDING COSTLY MISTAKES IN FINANCIAL DECISIONS

Many people sabotage their wealth by making poor financial choices. Whether it's rushing into investments without research or failing to plan for unexpected expenses, avoiding these mistakes is crucial for long-term success. Learning from the errors of others can help you make smarter financial decisions.

Common Financial Decision-Making Mistakes:

- Over-analyzing and Delaying Action: Waiting too long to make a move can cause missed opportunities.
- Ignoring Diversification: Putting all your money into one asset class increases risk and can lead to significant losses.
- Failing to Adjust to Market Changes: Being rigid with your financial plan instead of adapting to new trends can limit growth potential.

Action Step:

Review a past financial decision where you made a mistake. Write down what went wrong and how you can avoid making the same error in the future.

CHAPTER 28: HOW TO TURN SETBACKS INTO FINANCIAL COMEBACKS
THE POWER OF RESILIENCE IN WEALTH BUILDING

Financial setbacks are inevitable, but how you respond to them determines your future success. Every wealthy person has faced failures, but they use those experiences as lessons rather than stopping points. A strong mindset and strategic approach can turn financial losses into long-term gains.

Ways to Develop Financial Resilience:

- Reframe Failure as a Lesson: View every setback as an opportunity to learn and grow rather than a defeat.
- Have an Emergency Fund: A financial cushion can help you recover from unexpected losses without long-term damage.
- Surround Yourself with Resilient Thinkers: Being around people who have overcome obstacles can inspire and guide you.

Action Step:

Reflect on a past financial setback. Write down what you learned from it and how you can apply those lessons to future decisions.

STRATEGIES FOR BOUNCING BACK FROM FINANCIAL LOSSES

A major financial loss doesn't have to mean the end of wealth-building. Many successful entrepreneurs and investors have lost everything at some point, only to rebuild bigger and stronger. Implementing the right strategies can help you recover faster and avoid repeating the same mistakes.

Steps to Rebuild After a Financial Setback:

- Assess the Damage: Get a clear understanding of your current financial situation and where adjustments need to be made.
- Cut Unnecessary Expenses: Reduce spending while you work on regaining stability.
- Find New Income Sources: Look for new earning opportunities, whether through freelancing, side hustles, or higher-paying jobs.

Action Step:

If you've recently faced a financial loss, create a 90-day recovery plan outlining steps to reduce expenses, increase income, and regain financial stability.

STORIES OF COMEBACKS FROM FINANCIAL HARDSHIPS

Many of the world's most successful people have overcome massive financial hardships before achieving wealth. From bankruptcy to failed businesses, their resilience led them to financial success. Learning from their journeys can inspire and provide valuable insights for your own financial recovery.

Famous Comeback Stories:

- Elon Musk: Went nearly broke after investing everything into Tesla and SpaceX but rebounded to become one of the world's richest individuals.
- Walt Disney: Declared bankruptcy before launching the Disney empire, proving that failure isn't the end.
- Oprah Winfrey: Overcame financial struggles in her early career to build a billion-dollar media empire.

Action Step:

Research a successful person who has overcome financial hardship. Study their strategies and apply at least one of their lessons to your own financial journey.

CHAPTER 29: BUILDING WEALTH THROUGH COMMODITIES AND PRECIOUS METALS

WHY COMMODITIES CAN BE A SMART WEALTH-BUILDING STRATEGY

Investing in commodities like gold, silver, and oil has been a reliable hedge against inflation for centuries. During economic downturns, commodities often retain or increase their value, making them a great diversification tool. Billionaires like Ray Dalio advocate for holding a portion of wealth in commodities to protect against financial instability.

Types of Commodities for Wealth Building:

- Gold & Silver: Used as a store of value during economic crises.
- Oil & Natural Gas: Essential for global energy production.
- Agricultural Goods: Crops and livestock sustain global economies.

Action Step:

Research historical trends in commodity prices and consider allocating a small percentage of your portfolio to commodities.

HOW TO INVEST IN COMMODITIES

There are multiple ways to invest in commodities, including physical ownership, ETFs, and futures contracts. Legendary investor Jim Rogers built his fortune through commodity investments, proving their long-term profitability. The key is understanding market cycles and choosing commodities that align with economic trends.

Ways to Invest in Commodities:

- Physical Assets: Buying gold, silver, or other metals directly.
- Commodity ETFs: Investing in funds that track commodity prices.
- Futures & Options: High-risk, high-reward trading strategies.

Action Step:

Choose one method of commodity investment that aligns with your risk tolerance and financial goals.

RISKS AND STRATEGIES FOR MAXIMIZING COMMODITY INVESTMENTS

While commodities can be a powerful investment, they are subject to market volatility. Understanding geopolitical events, supply and demand, and inflation trends is crucial for maximizing returns. Smart investors hedge their risks by diversifying their portfolios across multiple asset classes.

Risk Management in Commodities

- Diversification: Don't invest solely in one commodity.
- Long-Term Holding: Commodities are better for wealth preservation than quick profits.
- Market Research: Stay updated on economic trends affecting commodity prices

Action Step:

Set a goal to track commodity price movements for the next three months to identify trends before investing.

CHAPTER 30: MASTERING WEALTH THROUGH PRIVATE EQUITY AND VENTURE CAPITAL

HOW PRIVATE EQUITY AND VENTURE CAPITAL CREATE WEALTH

Private equity and venture capital firms invest in early-stage and established businesses to scale them for high returns. Many of the world's richest investors, including Warren Buffett and Peter Thiel, have made billions through these investment strategies. By participating in these opportunities, investors can access higher returns than traditional stock markets.

Types of Private Equity & Venture Capital Investments:

- Startup Investing: High-growth companies with massive potential.
- Buyouts: Acquiring undervalued businesses and turning them around.
- Distressed Assets: Investing in struggling companies for long-term profit.

Action Step:

Research top venture capital firms and the industries they focus on to understand where money is flowing.

HOW TO GET STARTED IN PRIVATE EQUITY

While traditionally reserved for institutional investors, private equity opportunities are becoming more accessible to individuals. Platforms like AngelList allow retail investors to participate in startup funding rounds with smaller investments. Understanding deal structures and exit strategies is crucial for success.

Ways to Get Involved in Private Equity:

- Angel Investing: Small investments in early-stage startups.
- Private Equity Funds: Pooling capital with other investors.
- Direct Business Acquisitions: Buying and growing existing businesses.

Action Step:

Explore online platforms that provide access to private equity deals and consider making a small test investment.

RISK AND REWARD IN PRIVATE EQUITY INVESTING

Private equity offers higher returns than public stocks but also carries greater risks. The failure rate of startups is high, so diversification across multiple deals is essential. Smart investors balance private equity with safer, long-term investments for a secure portfolio.

Risk Management in Private Equity:

- Portfolio Diversification: Spread investments across multiple startups or funds.
- Due Diligence: Research company leadership, market fit, and financials.
- Long-Term Focus: Private equity requires patience for high returns.

Action Step:

If interested in private equity, start by networking with investors who have experience in this space to learn from their successes and mistakes.

CHAPTER 31: WEALTH-BUILDING THROUGH COLLECTIBLES AND ALTERNATIVE ASSETS

HOW COLLECTIBLES CAN BE A LUCRATIVE INVESTMENT

Rare collectibles such as vintage watches, art, classic cars, and sports memorabilia have outperformed traditional investments in certain periods. In 2021, a Honus Wagner baseball card sold for $6.6 million, showing the high-value potential of collectible assets. Investing in the right collectibles can generate significant wealth over time.

Types of Valuable Collectibles:

- Fine Art: Pieces by renowned artists appreciate over time.
- Classic Cars: Rare and vintage models hold long-term value.
- Luxury Watches: Rolex and Patek Philippe timepieces often increase in worth.

Action Step:

Research the appreciation trends of collectibles that interest you and track recent sales for price insights.

HOW TO START INVESTING IN COLLECTIBLES

The key to collectible investing is understanding rarity, demand, and authenticity. Platforms like Sotheby's and Christie's offer transparency for high-end collectibles, while alternative marketplaces make it easier for smaller investors to get started.

How to Start with Collectibles

- Focus on Passion & Knowledge: Invest in what you understand.
- Buy from Reputable Sources: Avoid counterfeits and scams.
- Hold for Long-Term Value: Patience is key for high returns.

Action Step:

Pick one category of collectibles and start learning about pricing trends, auctions, and market demand.

RISKS AND REWARDS OF COLLECTIBLE INVESTING

While collectibles can be lucrative, their value depends on market trends and buyer demand. Unlike stocks or real estate, they don't generate passive income, so liquidity can be a challenge. Successful investors focus on long-term appreciation and market timing.

Managing Risks in Collectible Investing:

- Storage & Insurance: Protect assets from damage or theft.
- Market Timing: Buy when demand is low, sell when it's high.
- Liquidity Considerations: Be prepared for longer holding periods.

Action Step:

If you're serious about collectible investing, attend a live auction or marketplace event to understand how pricing and demand work in real time.

CHAPTER 32: WEALTH CREATION THROUGH MEDIA AND CONTENT MONETIZATION

HOW CONTENT CAN BECOME A WEALTH-BUILDING MACHINE

With the rise of digital media, content creators can build massive income streams. YouTubers like MrBeast and podcasters like Joe Rogan have turned content into multimillion-dollar businesses. Creating valuable, engaging content can generate wealth through ads, sponsorships, and direct audience support.

Ways to Make Money from Content:

- YouTube Monetization: Earn from ads, memberships, and sponsorships.
- Podcasting: Advertising and listener support create income.
- Blogging & Newsletters: Subscription models and affiliate marketing generate profits.

Action Step:

Identify a content platform that aligns with your interests and start brainstorming niche ideas.

THE BUSINESS OF CONTENT CREATION

Successful content creators treat their platforms like businesses. Consistency, audience engagement, and multiple revenue streams are key to long-term profitability. Many influencers reinvest earnings to scale their brands into full-fledged companies.

Key Content Monetization Strategies:

- Diversified Income Streams: Use ads, sponsorships, and digital products.
- Audience Growth Techniques: Social media, SEO, and collaborations.
- Building a Loyal Community: Engagement leads to higher earnings.

Action Step:

Choose one platform and commit to posting consistently for 90 days.

CHAPTER 33: THE WEALTH MINDSET OF BILLIONAIRES

HOW BILLIONAIRES THINK DIFFERENTLY ABOUT MONEY

Billionaires don't just work for money–they make money work for them. Instead of focusing on saving every dollar, they prioritize scalable investments, ownership, and high-impact decision-making. A study by Thomas C. Corley, author of Rich Habits, found that 88% of self-made millionaires spend at least 30 minutes a day reading about success, finances, and self-improvement.

Key Wealth-Building Mentalities:

- Ownership Over Wages: The wealthy focus on owning assets–businesses, stocks, and real estate–rather than relying on a paycheck.
- Calculated Risk-Taking: Instead of fearing failure, they see risk as a necessary step toward exponential growth.
- Long-Term Vision: They invest in businesses and assets that compound over decades rather than seeking quick wins.

Action Step:

Identify one area in your life where you can shift from an employee mindset to an ownership mindset. Whether it's starting a business or investing, commit to making that shift this year.

THE POWER OF LEVERAGING NETWORKS AND RESOURCES

Ultra-wealthy individuals understand that success is rarely a solo journey. They build strategic partnerships, seek mentorship, and surround themselves with like-minded, successful individuals. Studies show that 79% of millionaires believe networking was critical to their success, as highlighted in the book The Millionaire Mindset by T. Harv Eker.

How Billionaires Build Their Inner Circle:

- Seek Mentorship: Jeff Bezos, Elon Musk, and Mark Zuckerberg all had mentors guiding them.
- Join Elite Masterminds: Warren Buffett credits much of his success to the people he surrounded himself with early in his career.
- Collaborate with Experts: The wealthy leverage partnerships to scale their businesses faster.

Action Step:

Reach out to one successful individual in your field this week–whether through LinkedIn, email, or networking events.

HOW BILLIONAIRES USE TIME DIFFERENTLY

One of the most valuable assets billionaires manage is their time. They delegate low-value tasks, automate processes, and focus only on decisions that generate the highest returns. Bill Gates once said, “Your most valuable resource is your time.”

Time Optimization Strategies of the Wealthy:

- Delegate Low-ROI Tasks: Outsource anything that doesn’t contribute to long-term wealth.
- Prioritize Learning: Billionaires spend hours each week reading, thinking, and strategizing.
- Leverage Automation: They use technology to streamline business and personal finance management.

Action Step:

Audit how you spend your time daily. Identify at least one task you can delegate or automate to free up time for higher-value activities.

CHAPTER 34: THE FUTURE OF WEALTH: AI, CRYPTO, AND EMERGING TECHNOLOGIES

HOW AI AND AUTOMATION ARE RESHAPING WEALTH

Artificial intelligence and automation are revolutionizing the way people build and grow wealth. AI-driven investment algorithms, automated businesses, and machine learning advancements are providing new financial opportunities. According to McKinsey, AI-driven decision-making is expected to contribute $13 trillion to the global economy by 2030.

How AI is Creating New Wealth-Building Avenues:

- AI-Powered Investing: Robo-advisors like Wealthfront and Betterment manage portfolios efficiently with minimal human involvement.
- Automated Businesses: AI-driven customer service, sales, and content creation are replacing traditional business models.
- Predictive Analytics for Finance: AI helps predict stock trends, crypto price movements, and market shifts.

Action Step:

Research at least one AI-driven financial tool that can enhance your investing or business strategies.

THE RISE OF CRYPTOCURRENCY AND DIGITAL ASSETS

Blockchain technology and digital currencies have redefined wealth-building strategies. While crypto is volatile, early investors in Bitcoin, Ethereum, and NFTs have seen unprecedented returns. A study by CoinDesk found that over 60% of millionaires under 40 have invested in digital assets.

Crypto Wealth Strategies:

- Diversified Crypto Portfolios: Smart investors don't go all-in on one coin–they spread risk across Bitcoin, Ethereum, and altcoins.
- Yield Farming & Staking: Passive income opportunities exist in DeFi (decentralized finance) platforms.
- Tokenized Assets: The future may include tokenized real estate, stocks, and business ownership.

Action Step:

If you haven't already, allocate a small percentage of your portfolio to digital assets after thorough research.

INVESTING IN THE NEXT BIG THING BEFORE IT HAPPENS

Wealthy investors don't chase trends–they identify them before they explode. Spotting emerging technologies and investing early is how people like Peter Thiel (Facebook's first investor) and Cathie Wood (Tesla investor) made billions.

How to Spot the Next Big Investment Opportunity:

- Follow Venture Capital Trends: Pay attention to what firms like Andreessen Horowitz and Sequoia Capital are funding.
- Watch for Industry Disruption: Innovations in biotech, space travel, and quantum computing may be the next wealth creators.
- Be Willing to Take Small Risks: Many successful investors allocate a small percentage of their portfolio to emerging sectors.

Action Step:

Research one emerging technology that interests you and explore ways to get involved as an investor, entrepreneur, or early adopter.

CHAPTER 35: THE ULTIMATE WEALTH FORMULA – YOUR PERSONALIZED PATH TO FINANCIAL FREEDOM

WEALTH IS PERSONAL – DEFINE YOUR OWN SUCCESS

Wealth isn't just about a number–it's about designing a life of financial freedom, security, and fulfillment. The richest people in the world aren't just chasing money; they're aligning wealth with their purpose. Studies by Harvard Business School have found that people who pursue financial goals tied to personal meaning report higher happiness levels than those who chase money for status alone.

How to Define Your Wealth Goals:

- What Does Wealth Mean to You? Is it financial independence, legacy, or the freedom to travel the world?
- Set a Concrete Wealth Goal: Whether it's $1 million in assets or $10K/month in passive income, clarity is key.
- Create a Vision Plan: Design your wealth strategy based on your skills, interests, and resources.

Action Step:

Write down your personal definition of wealth and set one actionable goal toward achieving it this year.

THE ULTIMATE WEALTH BLUEPRINT – THE STEPS THAT MATTER MOST

Throughout this book, you've learned strategies from investing to entrepreneurship to mindset shifts. Now, it's time to create a step-by-step plan tailored to your life.

The Core Steps to Building Wealth:

- Earn More: Increase income through high-income skills, businesses, and investments.
- Save & Invest Wisely: Grow your money through stocks, real estate, and passive income.
- Optimize & Protect Your Assets: Use tax strategies, trusts, and smart financial planning.
- Leverage & Scale: Use automation, networking, and technology to accelerate wealth-building.

Action Step:

Choose the top three strategies that resonate most with you and create a 12-month action plan to implement them.

YOUR WEALTH JOURNEY STARTS NOW

You now have the knowledge and strategies to create lasting financial success. The only thing left to do is take action. Every millionaire and billionaire started somewhere–what set them apart was consistency and execution.

Final Thoughts on Achieving Wealth:

- Action Beats Perfection: You don't need the perfect plan–start small and adjust as you go.
- Mindset is Everything: The difference between financial struggle and success is often mental.
- Never Stop Learning: Wealth-building is a lifelong process. Keep evolving and adapting.

Action Step:

Commit to taking action on at least one key wealth-building strategy today. Whether it's starting a side hustle, investing your first $100, or reading a financial book, begin now.

YOUR NEXT STEPS TO FINANCIAL FREEDOM

Reading this book is just the beginning. The real transformation happens when you take action.

1. Pick Three Wealth Strategies: Choose three key strategies from this book that resonate with you the most. Whether it's investing in real estate, building a digital product, or creating multiple income streams–commit to them.
2. Set a 12-Month Action Plan: Write down specific, measurable financial goals you want to achieve in the next year. Break them down into monthly action steps.
3. Take Immediate Action: Whether it's investing your first $100, starting a side hustle, or eliminating a financial drain–start today. Action creates momentum, and momentum creates results.
4. Surround Yourself with Success: Connect with like-minded individuals, join masterminds, and seek mentors who are already where you want to be.
5. Stay Consistent and Adapt: Wealth-building is a lifelong journey. There will be obstacles, market shifts, and unexpected challenges. The key is to stay adaptable and keep pushing forward.

CONCLUSION: YOUR WEALTH JOURNEY STARTS NOW

Wealth is not built overnight, nor is it achieved by luck. It is a result of strategic decisions, disciplined action, and an unshakable mindset. Throughout this book, you've gained insights into the most powerful wealth-building strategies, from investing and entrepreneurship to mastering negotiation and leveraging emerging technologies. But knowledge alone won't make you rich–execution will.

Every successful wealth-builder, from self-made millionaires to billionaires, started where you are today–with a decision. A decision to take control of their financial future, to stop making excuses, and to commit to a path of continuous growth. You now have the tools, strategies, and knowledge to build lasting wealth. The question is: what will you do with it?

Final Words: This is Your Moment

Most people dream of financial freedom, but only a few take action. You've already taken a step that 99% of people never will–educating yourself on the principles of wealth. Now, it's time to move from learning to doing. The path to wealth is in front of you. Will you take it? Your journey starts now.

Go build the wealth and life you deserve.

REFERENCES

- Mischel, Walter. The Marshmallow Test: Mastering Self-Control. Little, Brown and Company, 2014.
- Benartzi, Shlomo. Save More Tomorrow: Practical Behavioral Finance Solutions. University of California, 2012.
- Deloitte. Diversifying Income Streams: Financial Success Strategies of High-Net-Worth Individuals. Deloitte Insights, 2020.
- Dweck, Carol S. Mindset: The New Psychology of Success. Random House, 2006.
- Harvard Business Review. "Successful Angel Investors: How Due Diligence Improves Investment Outcomes." Harvard Business Review, 2018.
- McKinsey & Company. The Economic Impact of AI: $13 Trillion Market Growth by 2030. McKinsey Global Institute, 2020.

- Mischel, Walter. The Marshmallow Test: Mastering Self-Control. Little, Brown and Company, 2014.

- NerdWallet. "The Cost of Credit Card Debt in America." NerdWallet Finance Report, 2021.
- Stanley, Thomas J., and William D. Danko. The Millionaire Next Door: The Surprising Secrets of America's Wealthy. Longstreet Press, 1996.
- University of California, Berkeley. Angel Investment Returns: A Study of Early-Stage Startups. UC Berkeley Business Review, 2021.
- Upwork. Freelancing in the U.S. 2020. Upwork Research Reports, 2020.
- U.S. Small Business Administration. Franchise Business Loans and Their Success Rates. SBA.gov, 2022.
- Xiao, Jing J., and Barbara O'Neill. "Personal Finance Education: A Literature Review." Journal of Financial Counseling and Planning, vol. 27, no. 1, 2016, pp. 13-26.

www.ingramcontent.com/pod-product-compliance
Lightning Source LLC
LaVergne TN
LVHW100329210926
848480LV00003B/1297
9798348539092